MINNESOTA

SMITHMARK

This edition first published in 1992 by SMITHMARK
Publishers Inc., 112 Madison Avenue,
New York, New York 10016

ISBN 0-8317-0266-4

Printed and bound in Spain

Writer: Debra Ellen DeSalvo
Design Concept: Lesley Ehlers
Designer: Ann-Louise Lipman
Editor: Sara Colacurto
Production: Valerie Zars
Photo Researcher: Edward Douglas
Assistant Photo Researcher: Robert V. Hale
Editorial Assistant: Carol Raguso

Title page: Fishing is excellent in
Minnesota, whether you're fly-fishing in
a forest stream or trolling for muskies,
northern pike, or trout on one of the state's
15,291 lakes. *Opposite:* A strongly colored
totem pole climbs into the arctic air of
International Falls, a town on the
Canadian border that registers the lowest
winter temperatures in the United States.

Sky-blue water, crisp air, and hardy people are the hallmarks of Minnesota, the North Star state. So laced with lakes as to make a definitive count impossible, Minnesota is bigger, colder, and wetter than almost any other U.S. state. Proclaimed the "land of 10,000 lakes" on state license plates, it has over 15,000 at last count—several hundred more than Wisconsin, its neighbor to the east, can claim, despite a running argument.

Water covers one-twentieth of Minnesota's surface and forms many of its boundaries. Roughly defining the state's rectangular shape are the Red River to the west, the Minnesota River to the south, the St. Croix River to the east, and the Rainy and Pigeon rivers on the Canadian border. Further gracing that boundary from Lake of the Woods to Lake Superior is a string of sparkling wilderness lakes. Lake Itasca in the northwest region of the state is the source of the Mississippi River, which journeys 2,500 miles south to the Gulf of Mexico.

Most of Minnesota was covered at one time with glaciers, and the surface of the land was shaped by their movement and melting. The evidence of this prehistoric shifting is the thousands of lakes, most of which cover more than 10 acres each. Much of prehistoric Minnesota was in fact one enormous lake, the ancient Lake

Preceding pages: Daylight fades over Lake Kabetogama in Voyageurs National Park, named for the French Canadian *voyageurs* who used the string of 30 lakes in the park as a water highway between Lake Superior and Lake of the Woods. *Opposite:* Retreating glaciers formed Minnesota's many lakes and hewed sheer rock cliffs. *This page:* Sunset over Lake Superior at Superior National Forest, a three-million-acre forest stretching along the Minnesota–Canada border. Motor boats are banned from the forest's Boundary Waters Canoe area, one million acres of several thousand lakes linked by short portages.

Agriculture remains the state's largest business, but it flourishes primarily on the large farms in southern Minnesota; many northern family farms have suffered foreclosures in the past two decades. *Opposite:* Vibrant fall foliage as seen from Oberg Mountain in Superior National Forest.

Agassiz, an inland sea far larger than all the Great Lakes combined. It covered 110 thousand miles of Minnesota, North Dakota, and Manitoba and found its outlet—the glacial River Warren—where today's Dakota boundaries meet the Minnesota state line.

As it drained Lake Agassiz, the Warren carved the wide valley of what is now the Minnesota River. As the Ice Age waned, the lake retreated northward, leaving behind the rich farmland of the Red River Valley. The Warren channel remains, framing the narrow, lazy Minnesota River in a wide, loam-covered valley that cuts into the western prairies and across the lake-strewn land like the imprint of a boomerang.

At the confluence of the broad Mississippi and the twisting Minnesota River lie the Twin Cities of Minneapolis and St. Paul. Some say Minnesota is really two states: the Twin Cities and their sprawling suburbs, where more than half the people of the state live without feeling crowded, and the rest of Minnesota—farms, forests, lakes, and small towns.

The rash of farm foreclosures in the 1970's and 1980's served to push the two groups even further apart, for the Twin Cities steadily grew while much of the rest of the state lost population. Conflicts are often fought out in the state capitol in St. Paul between rural legislators fearful that Minneapolis and St. Paul are prospering at the expense

Top to bottom: The Grand Portage is a nine-mile trail that was used by fur traders in the 1700's to bypass the 20 miles of falls and rapids they would have had to navigate if they had stayed waterbound. The North West Company established a post at the mouth of the Pigeon River on Lake Superior, which has been reconstructed as the Grand Portage National Monument. The stockade, great hall, and kitchen capture the flavor of wilderness life. *Opposite:* The rising sun glints off rocky Palisade Head on the north shore of Lake Superior.

Dawn illuminates bedrock and pools at Grand Marais, a natural harbor and the ideal starting point for a foray into Superior National Forest.

Icy water sprays and foams off the rocky coast of Lake Superior, the world's largest freshwater lake.

of their constituents and city
politicians, many of whom believe
the main goal of their country
counterparts is to impede the
cities' efforts to solve their urban
growing pains.

Although one in four
Minnesotans have Scandinavian
blood, more than 60 ethnic groups
have emigrated to the state since
the early 1800's. The earliest
migrants were Dakota (Sioux)
and Ojibway (Chippewa) Indians,
both of whom had well-established
societies when a French procession
planted a white flag embroidered
with the gold fleur-de-lis into the
black soil of the Minnesota River
Valley in 1689.

French fur traders were followed by English ones, until both
were routed in the aftermath of
the American Revolution. The
American government established
Fort Snelling at the mouth of the
Mississippi River in 1819, where
it still stands. From then until
about 1890, the people who chose
the fertile land and harsh
winters of Minnesota emigrated
principally from northern and
western Europe. The early
Minnesotan mosaic was com-
posed of Germans, Scandinavians,
Poles, and Finns, as well as
Yankees of English, Welsh, and
Irish extraction. Next came
skilled dairy farmers from
Holland and Denmark.

The opening of the mighty
Mesabi iron range and the
development of the railways
brought hardworking Russians,

The Split Rock Lighthouse looks out
over Lake Superior's seemingly endless
expanse. The 54-foot octagonal lighthouse
was built atop a 100-foot bluff in 1910.
Its light still warns ships away from the
treacherous coast. *Opposite:* Water, wind,
and ice have carved the northern shore of
Lake Superior.

Ice floes on Agate Bay make it difficult for ships to enter Two Harbors, the Lake Superior iron port comprising Agate Bay and Burlington Bay. *Below, left:* The same icy conditions that render Agate Bay unapproachable create a winter wonderland in Manitou Falls. *Right:* Two present-day travelers experience the same awe that Native Americans, English explorers, and *voyageurs* must have felt when passing under this massive rock arch.

White birches cling to the thin topsoil on the sheer bedrock cliffs towering over Lake Superior at Tettegouche State Park.

Slovaks, Slovenes, Croats, Serbs, Bulgars, Romanians, Italians, and Greeks to Minnesota to dig for ore and populate the new urban and industrial centers of the early 1900's. Germans and Scandinavians continued to pour in, with more Norwegians arriving between 1900 and 1909 than in any previous decade. Germans, Swedes, and Norwegians comprise the three largest ethnic groups in the state.

Migrant Mexican field workers brought north to cull the sugar beet fields began to settle in St. Paul in the 1930's and were followed into the Twin Cities by Europe's fleeing World War II refugees—Estonians, Latvians, Lithuanians, Hungarians, Ukrainians, Czechs, and Poles.

Middle Eastern and Asian communities formed in Minnesota between 1890 and 1920, paving the way for the Chinese, Japanese, Filipino, Korean, Indochinese, and Arabic people who streamed into the state after World War II. Early immigrants came to work the railroads and the mines; later many came to attend the University of Minnesota. Refugees from Southeast Asia found their way to the Twin Cities in the late 1970's. By 1980 the metropolis had the largest single settlement of Hmong people in the United States and also supported pockets of Laotians and Cambodians.

Top: Stocking up for a fishing expedition into Superior National Forest is easy in the bustling little village of Grand Marais. *Left:* The history of the Arrowhead region is intertwined with the exploitation of the great iron ranges and is preserved in detail at Ironworld USA.

International freighters enter Duluth-Superior Harbor to unload their goods at the world's largest ore docks and grain elevators. The development of the iron ranges turned Duluth into a prosperous and powerful city; by the 1950's Minnesota was producing 82% of the nation's iron ore and shipping much of it out through Duluth-Superior Harbor.

The entire floor of the delicate-looking Aerial Lift Bridge can be raised 138 feet in less than a minute to let ships into Duluth-Superior Harbor. *Below:* "Skywalks" such as Medical Skyway in Duluth prevent frostbite during Minnesota's harsh winters. *Opposite:* A modern lighthouse stands ready to illuminate the darkening sky over Lake Superior.

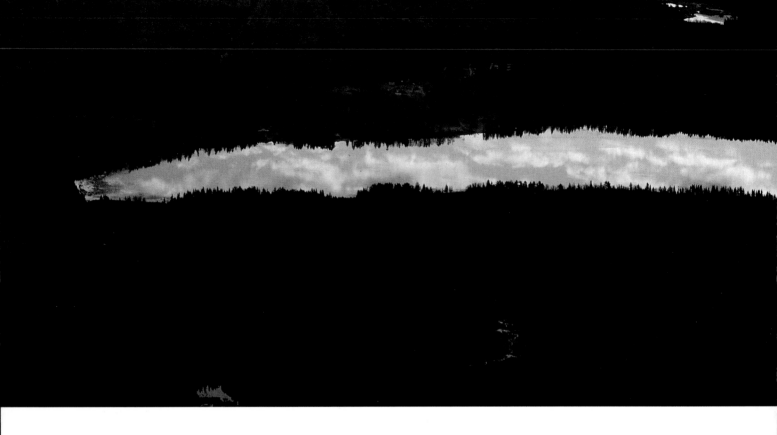

The Mississippi River begins at the shining waters of Lake Itasca. Here the great muddy river is clear and so narrow one can step right across it.

Although racial tensions exacerbated by economic recessions rose, families, congregations, and civic groups responded compassionately to the emergency needs of the Indochinese refugees. Indochinese New Year celebrations and cultural events are now interwoven into the fabric of Twin Cities life and add spice to the northern European stew.

Slightly more than 1 percent of Minnesota's population is black, about 90 percent of whom live in the Twin Cities. The Native American population of around 35,000 is primarily Ojibway; the Sioux were banished following their uprising in 1862. A third of the state's Native Americans are concentrated in the Twin Cities, the remainder living on scattered reservations.

The history of the settlement of Minnesota is the story of two great races—red and white— who lived together in peace for centuries until the Great Sioux Uprising of 1862. Until the mid-nineteenth century, the Ojibway held the north and east of the area, while the Dakota occupied the south and west. But tribes from as far away as the Appalachians and the Rocky Mountains met in a sacred place of peace in southwestern Minnesota to quarry a soft red rock for peace pipes; this quarry is preserved today as the Pipestone National Monument. The stone is now protected, and in summer craftspeople come to work with it at The Upper Midwest Indian Cultural Center.

Top: This 26-foot statue of Paul Bunyan, the legendary lumberjack, and his 15-foot companion, Babe the Blue Ox, in Bemidji are reputedly the most-photographed statues in the United States. *Right:* Bemidji, birthplace of Paul Bunyan, was a booming logging town in the late 1800's and is now a popular tourist attraction featuring steamboat rides and the Bunyan House Information Center.

Preceding pages: The waving grasses of the Tall Grass Prairie are the setting for
the stories Laura Ingalls Wilder wrote that became the "Little House on the Prairie"
TV series. The Dakota Indians considered the prairie region near the South Dakota
stateline the sacred home of their ancestors. "Fish in the box!" is the proud cry
of the successful fisher, in this instance a Lake Mille Lacs fishing guide with a
couple of walleye. *This page:* Dock, reeds, and boat throw brushstroke silhouettes
against the setting summer sun on Lake Mille Lacs.

Preceding page: The repeating arches of Central Avenue Bridge lead the eye to downtown Minneapolis at dusk. *This page, right:* Minneapolis's first skyscraper, the 447-foot-high Foshay Tower, was the tallest building in the upper Midwest for decades. *Below:* Three miles of modern skyway, such as this one crossing over Hennepin Avenue, weave through downtown Minneapolis, allowing citizens to go about their business even when it's 50 degrees below zero.

The Kensington Stone, discovered in west central Minnesota in 1898, bears what until recently were believed to be Norse runes from the fourteenth century. However, it now appears to be a clever forgery; the earliest known Europeans in the area were actually seventeenth-century French explorers hunting for the Northwest Passage. The first white settlement was made by French fur traders leaving Lake Superior to make a nine-mile portage around the falls and rapids of the Pigeon River. It was these French *voyageurs* who named the Dakota people *Sioux,* from *Nadouesse,* meaning "snake in the grass," the unkind epithet given them by their enemies, the Ojibway. The Ojibway had by then forced the Sioux out of the northern forest to the Minnesota Valley.

To Europeans seeking a fresh start in an abundant land, the Minnesota Valley was Eden. As the adventurer Captain Jonathan Carver wrote in 1767, the Minnesota River "flows through a most delightful country, abounding with all the necessaries of life, that grow spontaneously; and with a little cultivation it might be made to produce even the luxuries of life."

For many years fur traders and Native Americans coexisted peacefully and profitably, but the farmers drawn by the black soil of the ancient River Warren's

Top to bottom: The twin towers of the Pillsbury Building seem, from this vantage point, to be leaning together for a talk. The ultra-modern glassed curves of the Federal Reserve Bank building reflect the Minneapolis sky and are echoed in the pale orange sculpture on the plaza beneath it. While a prisoner of the Sioux Indians 300 years ago, the Belgian priest Father Louis Hennepin caught sight of a small waterfall outside of what is now Minneapolis and named it St. Anthony Falls in honor of his patron saint. *Opposite:* What at first appears to be a reflection is actually Minneapolis City Hall as seen through a huge window of the nearby Government Center.

channel wanted to own and tame the land. When the Territory of Minnesota was organized in 1849, the motto of the official seal was blunt: *Quae sursum volo videre,* "I fain would see what lies beyond." The seal was a drawing of a mounted Indian pursued by an armed farmer and his plow.

The fur traders, who had been dependent on the Sioux for so long, would have preferred to see the farmers turned back, but for the fact that the area was trapped out. Both game and fur animals were scarce by the mid-nineteenth century. The fur traders turned their attentions instead toward pushing the Sioux to sell land to the U.S. government, so the traders could claim that the natives owed them money and divert the purchase dollars to their own pockets.

In the summer of 1851, *voyageurs,* traders, government officials, farmers, and bands of valley Sioux, as well as representatives from other tribes, met at the mouth of the Minnesota River. On July 23, after several days of feasting, lacrosse, and even a wedding, Sleepy Eyes and 34 other Upper Sioux chiefs signed away 30 million acres in Iowa and Minnesota, retaining only a 20-mile strip as a reservation along the upper Minnesota River. The chiefs were to receive annual payments of $68,000 until the $1,665,000 purchase price was paid, minus $275,000 set aside to dispose of debts incurred by tribesmen for traders' goods. On August 5 at Mendota, the Mdewakanton and Wahpekute bands of Lower Sioux signed away most of the southeast quarter of the state for $1,410,000 in cash and annuities over 50 years.

The treaties left the 7,000 Sioux two reservations, each 20

Preceding page: The brightly painted walls of the Vaspar Corporation Building express the brash, exuberant spirit of Minneapolis. The youthful population encourages fresh approaches to the city's renovation. *This page:* The home of the Minnesota Vikings football team and baseball's Minnesota Twins is the Hubert H. Humphrey Metrodome.

The largest urban sculpture garden in the United States is the Minneapolis Sculpture Garden, opened by the Walker Arts Center in 1988. A walk among the garden's high hedges takes one past a variety of remarkable pieces, including the enormous *Spoonbridge and Cherry* fountain (above, left) by Claes Oldenburg and Coosje van Bruggen and Frank Gehry's sparkling *Standing Glass Fish* (above, right). The garden is linked to downtown by a footbridge.

Figures in a Paul Granlund sculpture raise their arms to the clean, spare lines of the Westminster Presbyterian Church in Minneapolis. *Below:* Delicate figures and a circle of stained-glass windows decorate the interior dome of Lakewood Chapel.

miles wide and about 70 miles long. The Upper Sioux considered their land, from Lake Traverse to the Yellow Medicine River, acceptable, as it included the sites of their old villages, but the Lower Sioux were dissatisfied with their domain, which was on the prairie about eight miles northwest of present-day New Ulm, far from their beloved forest. The Sioux also believed they had been cheated by the traders into signing away too much of their payments to cover debts.

By 1857, land-hungry settlers clamored for a further reduction of Sioux territory. In 1858, when Minnesota became the thirty-second state, several Sioux chiefs were tempted by promises of further annuity payments to sign away the strip of land along the north side of the Minnesota River, nearly a million acres. Congress agreed two years later to pay 30 cents an acre. After the usual traders' claims, the payment was cut in half.

The dangers of the government's policies concerning Native Americans were summed up in a letter to President Lincoln from Episcopal Bishop Henry B. Whipple in 1862 calling attention to fraud in the treaty system and advocating the abandonment of cash annuities, which flowed directly into traders' hands, and suggesting the government instead provide seeds, tools, and other commodities directly to the Sioux to support their tribal system.

Top: The Guthrie Theater, awarded a Tony in 1982 for its contribution to American theater, continues to present an invigorating mix of classic and avant-garde productions. *Left:* The Twin Cities are the cultural mecca of the Upper Great Lakes region; even Nicollet Mall, a mile-long pedestrian shopping district, offers Orchestra Hall on Peavey Plaza.

The 33-room château-style mansion now housing the American Swedish Institute was the fanciful creation of Swan J. Turnblad, publisher of one of the largest Swedish-language newspapers in the United States. *Below:* A wanderer through the Eloise Garden near Lake Harriet, one of the Minneapolis chain of lakes, might come across this fountain.

Whipple noted: "We have broken up, in part, their tribal relations and they must have something in their place."

The series of events leading to the Sioux Uprising of 1862 is complex, but the final straw was the refusal of traders at the Upper Sioux Agency to extend credit to hungry Sioux when the government annuity payment didn't arrive from Washington that August. Little Crow and his people waited over a week for money that didn't come; when the chief asked for food and was refused several times, he growled, "When men are hungry, they help themselves." Trader Andrew Myrick's storehouse was close to the agency, but he refused to extend credit, saying, "So far as I am concerned, if they are hungry, let them eat grass."

On the morning of August 18, Little Crow and his followers silently surrounded the stores, the barns, and the warehouse in the agency compound. The first target was Myrick's store; Myrick escaped, only to be found dead later in a field with grass stuffed into his mouth. The Sioux had decided to clear the valley of whites and went at it with a vengeance, aware that many of the region's soldiers were away at the Civil War. By the time newly appointed brigadier general Henry Sibley was able to assemble a few hundred troops, some 500 settlers were dead and more burned out of their homes. By mid-September he had pushed the Sioux out of the valley and Little Crow was dead, shot by a settler who surprised him in a berry patch near Hutchinson.

Enraged Minnesotans, not satisfied with the mass hanging of 38 Sioux after the uprising, called for banishment of the tribes from the state. Governor Ramsey declared on September 9, 1862, "The Sioux Indians of

Preceding page: When warm weather finally does arrive, Minnesotans can get a little nutty. If sculpting giant sand beetles isn't exciting enough, there's always the Aquatennial Milk Carton Boat Race on Lake Nokomis. Apparently some folks feel the need to pretend it's 50 below *all* the time. *This page:* Lakes and parks such as the charming Lake o' the Isles dot metropolitan Minneapolis, providing tranquil getaways within walking distance of downtown. *Following pages, left:* Standing above the waterfall mythologized in Longfellow's *The Song of Hiawatha* is a tender bronze depiction of Hiawatha and Minnehaha. *Right:* Minnehaha Falls spills into Minnehaha Creek, which runs along 15 miles of jogging, biking, and roller-skating trails that are very popular with Twin Cities residents.

"O'er wide and rushing rivers
In his arms he bore the maiden"
Longfellow

Preceding page: The stern expressions on the faces of these granite pioneers reflect the tenacity that was necessary for survival of fierce northern Minnesota winters. *This page:* Neon trails form a Saturnian ring around a ride at Valleyfair Amusement Park in Shakopee.

St. Paul is the Mississippi River-dominated half
of the Twin Cities—tugboats chug right through
downtown stringing grain barges together for trips
downstream. *Right:* The Mississippi River swings a
wide loop through St. Paul, giving the city 29 miles
of sparkling waterfront.

Whereas Minneapolis has been quick to tear down old buildings to make way for new skyscrapers, St. Paul has been careful to preserve its Victorian and Art Deco heritage while still making room for modern structures such as the St. Paul Companies Insurance Co.'s round tower (above, left) and the new World Trade Center (above, right). *Below:* In contrast to the brash colors and patterns spotted on some Minneapolis structures, St. Paul's architectural past is reflected in the gentle color schemes used to repaint buildings.

Minnesota must be exterminated or driven forever beyond the borders of the State."

With the banishment of the Sioux, farming took over, and by 1920 Minneapolis was the world's leading producer of flour. The discovery of iron ore in the Vermillion and Mesabi ranges in the 1880's and the exploitation of the timberland also fueled the state's growth. By 1951 Minnesota was producing 82 percent of the nation's iron ore, but during the late 1960's and early 1970's mining and lumbering fell off. Agriculture is now Minnesota's largest industry, employing one in three residents.

Most of the big dairy, grain, and cattle farms are located in southern Minnesota. The fertile countryside, dotted with lakes, stretches from the bluffs of the Mississippi River west across pastures and prairies to the South Dakota border. The river towns of Red Wing and Winona celebrate their steamboat days with paddle-wheel riverboat tours and festivals. When wheat was the top crop in the region, it was shipped through Winona, which today is headquarters for the 300-mile Upper Mississippi River National Wildlife and Fish Refuge. Further inland lies Rochester, home of the famed Mayo Clinic, whose 800 doctors are visited by over 200 thousand patients each year.

West of Rochester is Minneopa State Park, more than a thousand acres of scenic river valley and prairie lands and two gorgeous waterfalls. Only 30 miles northwest of the park is New Ulm, site of two of the most ferocious battles of the Great Sioux Uprising. From there visitors can continue west to the Pipestone area. Between Pipestone and New Ulm lies tiny

Preceding page, above: The 1892 Gothic-style Landmark Center and other buildings of that era surround Rice Park, a square-block park in the heart of downtown St. Paul that captures the city's old-world reserve. *Below:* The 20-story building housing City Hall and Ramsey County Courthouse was built in 1931 in a popular style of the day called American Perpendicular. *This page, above:* The Cathedral of St. Paul is modeled after St. Peter's of Rome—with one obvious exception being the statue commemorating the First Minnesota Infantry. *Below, left:* The golden horses and charioteer charging from the marble dome of the State Capitol building form a sculpture titled *The Progress of the State. Right:* Pink marble, Neo-Renaissance statues, and stained glass give the interior of the Cathedral of St. Paul its European flavor.

A glimpse of the top of St. Louis Catholic Church with Galtier Plaza towering over it (above) makes the church look insignificant when, in fact, it is quite imposing viewed from the ground (below).

A glorious fairytale castle made of ice rises high above the grounds of Winter Carnival in St. Paul. *Below:* Glowing ice totems and figures inhabit Rice Park; Landmark Center and bare winter trees are draped in lights.

An impenetrable ice fortress complete with flying flags (above) guards Harriet Island, a center of carnival activity, while an ice griffin (below) raises its wings threateningly.

Walnut Grove, home to Laura Ingalls Wilder, author of the stories on which the TV series "Little House on the Prairie" was based.

Southern Minnesota is mostly rolling prairie and productive farms, and offers fine lakes and excellent cross-country skiing. But when Minnesotans vacation they head toward the rugged northern part of the state, where cold streams rush past outcroppings of granite, which was thrust upward as the earth warmed at the end of the Ice Age. Northern Minnesota shelters two national forests, a string of lakes open only to canoes, and a national park.

The northeastern tip of the state is called the Arrowhead, because of its shape where it projects into Lake Superior. Here lie the three great Minnesotan iron ore ranges. At the bottom corner of the Arrowhead sprawls the seaport of Duluth, which sprang up to ship ore and grain and became—with its twin port of Superior, Wisconsin, across the bay—the second-busiest port in the nation. International Falls, on the Canadian border opposite Fort Francis, Ontario, is the coldest spot in the United States in the winter.

The Arrowhead's western counterpart is Vikingland, the far northwestern corner of Minnesota. The region is divided between flat Red River Valley land supporting huge wheat farms, similar to those of the Great Plains, and lakes, forests, and wildlife refuges. Many of its resorts offer the best inland lake fishing in the Midwest and much of the region's economy depends on tourism. The 61,000-acre Agassiz National Wildlife Refuge is the only mainland wildlife refuge to host a wolf pack; it is home to 41 mammal species and over 245 types of birds.

Preceding page, top to bottom: The 15 rooms of the house of the first governor of the Minnesota territory, Alexander Ramsey, have been restored to their original glamor. While he wrote *This Side of Paradise*, F. Scott Fitzgerald lived in one of the Victorian houses lining Summit Avenue, a four-and-a-half-mile street boasting the nation's longest intact row of Victorian residences. The enormous red sandstone home of James J. Hill, builder of the Great Northern Railroad, was completed in 1891. *This page:* The Como Park Conservatory shelters more than 200 species, as well as an adjacent traditional Japanese outdoor garden, sunken gardens, a fern room, and biblical plantings. Seasonal flower shows are a good excuse for Minnesotans to come in from the cold and smell the flowers.

Fort Snelling has watched over the junction of the Mississippi and Minnesota rivers since 1819. *Below:* The mellow St. Croix River defines the Minnesota–Wisconsin border from the Twin Cities north until it heads east into Wisconsin's half of the Interstate Park. *Opposite:* Snow covers the roofs of the old churches and renovated homes of historic Stillwater, situated just north of the Twin Cities on the St. Croix River.

Preceding page: The scarlet flowers running down the center of this flowerbed on Red Wing Historic Mall might be the same color as the "wing of the wild swan dyed scarlet" worn by Dakota Indian chiefs for whom Red Wing was named. *This page:* The stone facade over the entrance to the Mayo Clinic, which draws 200,000 patients a year to its complex in Rochester, sensitively expresses the hope these visitors bring with them.

Hardy Minnesota horses trot through a field of Queen Anne's lace past a barn obviously owned by a farmer with a sense of humor.

The fifth region of Minnesota is the Heartland, the strip reaching north from the Twin Cities to the Canadian border. The northern Heartland is Paul Bunyan country. Myth has it that the lumberjack and Babe the Blue Ox cleared the forests for the Scandinavian and German settlers who came to farm the land in the late nineteenth century. Lake Itasca, at the northern tip of the Heartland, gives birth to the Mississippi River, which runs into Minneapolis-St. Paul. The Twin Cities are certainly not identical and rarely act fraternal. The rivalry between the inhabitants of each is legendary. When major league sports teams began looking for a site, each city built a stadium, with the result that the Minnesota Vikings (football) and Twins (baseball) were the first teams to be named for a state instead of a city.

Although both cities have gleaming modern skyscrapers, St. Paul is quieter, older, and more reserved, while Minneapolis is hip and energetic, engendering not one but two distinct pop music movements: rock superstar Prince's funk/punk as well as the popular garage rock of The Replacements and Soul Asylum. Minneapolis boasts the state university—St. Paul has the capitol; proponents of each city could go on and on—and do! Perhaps it's best to simply point to the diversity and shifting fortunes of the Twin Cities as reflecting the same qualities in Minnesota's own landscape and people.

Top: The Schell Brewing wagon displays barrels of flowers at the New Ulm German Heritagefest parade; Schell has been around almost as long as New Ulm, which was established by Germans from Ulm in 1854. *Right:* Peggy DeMers and Marvin McCoy celebrate at the Heritagefest by blowing their alphorns.

Preceding page: Plain wooden crosses at a veterans memorial in Ivanhoe eloquently express the tragedy of young lives lost to war. *This page:* Soybean plants and the local church: two staples of modern Minnesotan farm life.

Pioneer Village in Worthington clearly understands the essentials of small-town life—the bank and the general store stand side by side on Main Street. *Left:* Fertile black topsoil rests under a blanket of snow while the denuded poplar trees that mark a farm's border extend their brittle branches to the silent winter sky.

Index of Photography

All photographs courtesy of The Image Bank, except where indicated *.

Page Number	Photographer	Page Number	Photographer
Title Page	Tim Bieber	35 Top	Greg Ryan/Sally Beyer*
3	Greg Ryan/Sally Beyer*	35 Bottom	Lou Bowman*
4-5	Greg Ryan/Sally Beyer*	36 Top	Greg Ryan/Sally Beyer*
6	Gerald Brimacombe	36 Bottom	Conrad Bloomquist*
7 Top	Richard Hamilton Smith*	37 Top	Andy Caulfield
7 Bottom	Gerald Brimacombe	37 Bottom	Greg Ryan/Sally Beyer*
8	Greg Ryan/Sally Beyer*	38 Top & Bottom	Steve Schneider*
9	Conrad Bloomquist*	38 Center	Conrad Bloomquist*
10 Top	Greg Ryan/Sally Beyer*	39	Richard Hamilton Smith*
10 Center & Bottom	John & Ann Mahan*	40	Conrad Bloomquist*
11	Greg Ryan/Sally Beyer*	41	Mike Magnuson*
12	Greg Ryan/Sally Beyer*	42	Greg Ryan/Sally Beyer*
13	Greg Ryan/Sally Beyer*	43	Greg Ryan/Sally Beyer*
14 (2)	Alvis Upitis	44-45 (2)	Nancy Bundt
15	Gerald Brimacombe	46 Top Left	Greg Ryan/Sally Beyer*
16 Top	Mike Magnuson*	46 Top Right	Kay Shaw*
16 Bottom Left	Gerald Brimacombe	46 Bottom	Richard Hamilton Smith*
16 Bottom Right	Richard Hamilton Smith*	47 Top	Conrad Bloomquist*
17	Greg Ryan/Sally Beyer*	47 Bottom	Greg Ryan/Sally Beyer*
18 (2)	Greg Ryan/Sally Beyer*	48 Top	Greg Ryan/Sally Beyer*
19 (2)	Richard Hamilton Smith*	48 Bottom Left	Jake Rajs
20 Top	Steve Schneider*	48 Bottom Right	Greg Ryan/Sally Beyer*
20 Bottom	Alvis Upitis	49 Top	Greg Ryan/Sally Beyer*
21	Alvis Upitis	49 Bottom	DC Productions
22 (2)	Jake Rajs	50 Top	Richard Hamilton Smith*
23 (2)	Greg Ryan/Sally Beyer*	50 Bottom	Kay Shaw*
24-25	Richard Hamilton Smith*	51 Top	Greg Ryan/Sally Beyer*
26	Greg Ryan/Sally Beyer*	51 Bottom	Kay Shaw*
27	Greg Ryan/Sally Beyer*	52 (3)	Alvis Upitis
28	Andy Caulfield	53 Top	Nancy Bundt
29 Top	Richard Hamilton Smith*	53 Bottom	Ed Bock/Frozen Images*
29 Bottom	Greg Ryan/Sally Beyer*	54 Top	Kay Shaw*
30 Top	Nancy Bundt	54 Bottom	Gerald Brimacombe
30 Center	Jake Rajs	55	Greg Ryan/Sally Beyer*
30 Bottom	Steve Schneider*	56	Conrad Bloomquist*
31	Richard Hamilton Smith*	57	Andy Caulfield
32 (2)	Jake Rajs	58	Conrad Bloomquist*
33	David Maenza	59 (2)	Greg Ryan/Sally Beyer*
34 Top Left	Andy Caulfield	60	Greg Ryan/Sally Beyer*
34 Top Right	Alvis Upitis	61	Greg Ryan/Sally Beyer*
34 Bottom	Jake Rajs	62-63 (2)	Jake Rajs